Rebellious and Almost Repentant

Leanne Neill
LUST for WORDS

Other books by Leanne Neill

Fine Lines and Unpolished Pieces of Me (2017)
Blue Lotus (2018).

Rebellious and Almost Repentant

Copyright © 2019 Leanne Neill
All Rights Reserved
ISBN 978-1-925332-51-3

Cover designed by
L. Neill and M. Gregory

Cover Image:
Shutterstock©Maisei Raman

Internal illustrations:
Shutterstock©Maisei Raman
(beads, heart.hands)
Shutterstock©1001holiday
(bustier)
Internal Photographs
Heart in sky © Voe Gillespie
All others © Leanne Neill

This book may not be reproduced, transmitted, or stored in whole or in part by any means, including graphic, electronic, or mechanical without the express written consent of the author except in the case of brief quotations embodied in critical articles and reviews and non-commercial uses permitted by copyright law.

For permission requests, address the request to the author c/o
Permissions,
jneill@bigpond.net.au

Printed in Australia

Publisher of record
Tried and Trusted Indie Publishing
www.tatindiepublishing.com

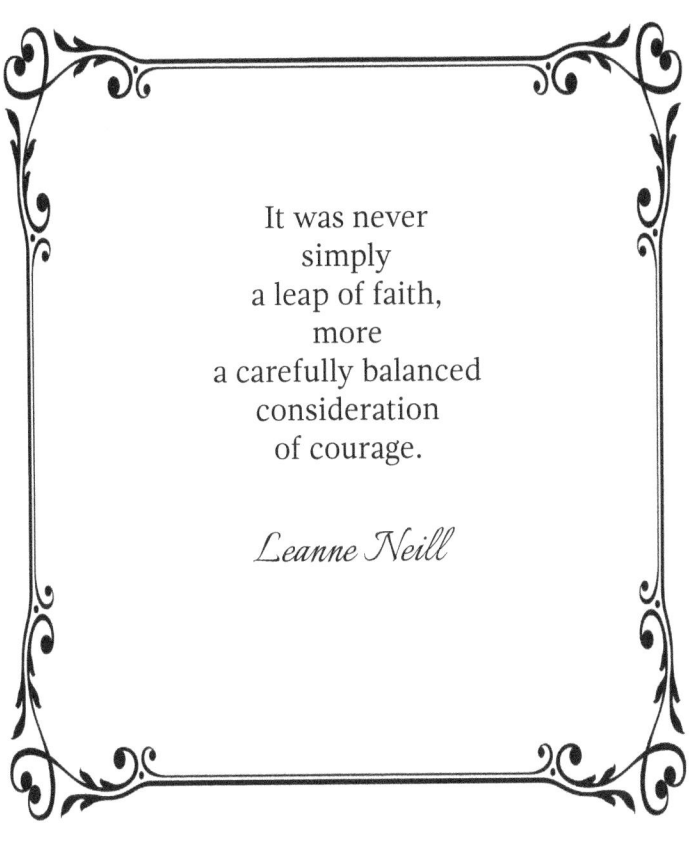

It was never
simply
a leap of faith,
more
a carefully balanced
consideration
of courage.

Leanne Neill

"I know her so well now that I have not the slightest idea
who she really is."
- *Gabriel Garcia Marquez*

PREFACE

I believe something happens to women from their late thirties onwards. An awareness of self, a coming of age, a period of questioning, a revolution. Our forties and fifties are a time of complete metamorphosis; our bodies transform from child carrying vessels into shells that threaten to echo. Society impinges upon our self-worth and esteem, yet we are burgeoning, ripening into exquisite, sometimes confused, super-powerful beings.

Often this time is under spoken; judgement is a fear we never entirely seem to lose. I'm putting it out there...in my own unique form. Rebellious and Almost Repentant concludes what I call my 'trilogy of mid-life madness.' Mostly new work, sprinkled with memorable pieces from *Fine Lines and Unpolished Pieces of Me* (2017) and *Blue Lotus* (2018).

As a girl I always dreamed I could be someone. I never imagined it could take a lifetime to know who it is.

Thank you.
Leanne X

ACKNOWLEDGEMENTS

For my children Caleb, Samuel and Charlotte,
for surviving with me as your mother.

To all women rebellious and almost repentant;
no need for apologies. X
To those men who continue to love them,
hats off and thank you! X

Special thanks to my biggest supporter and Rock of Gibraltar, Maddalena Ghayyoori, and my Creative Collaborator, Luisa Romeo.
To Robert, for the gift of remembering. XXX

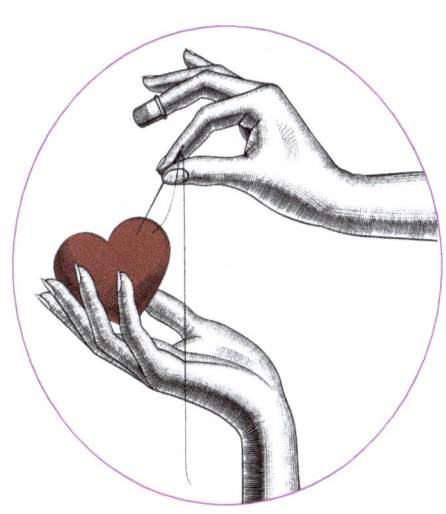

REBELLIOUS

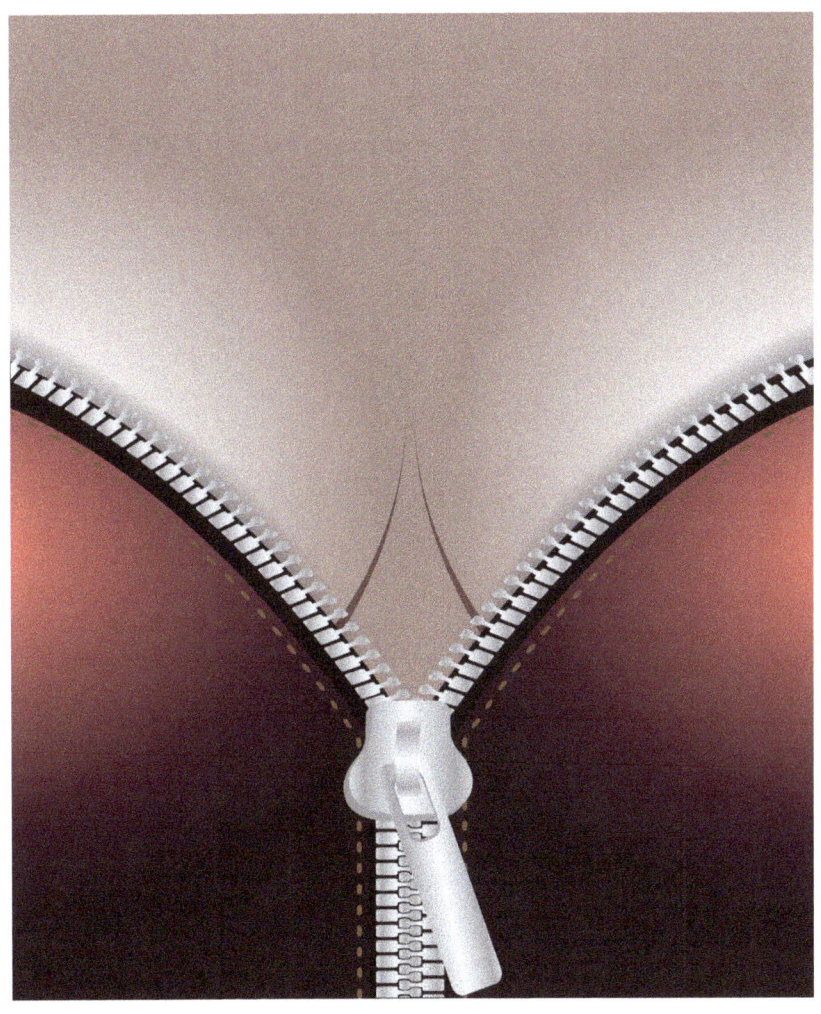

MID COLOUR CRISIS

She prays to purple
rain gods,
tattoos her skin
blue,
wears red lips
that show teeth white,
needles
her forehead pink,
refuses to yellow smile,
swallows a black lover,
takes a green pill,
any colour wine.

*If you're not practicing evolution of self,
you're procrastinating on poison apples.*

Rebellious

WRITTEN IN THE CARDS

Voodoo woman,
mystical knowledge;
flips animal cards for me –
I'm not an animal person...
(I suspect it's the faux-fur vest
I'm wearing!)
Draws a salmon card –
apparently, I'm likened to
a deep-sea fish...
I politely tell her
I do indeed enjoy salmon!
(Already, I'm quietly sniggering.)

Flip, flip...
Starts off well –
You are amazingly creative, aren't you?
Your power is in your hand.
Wow, I think,
I've struck the jackpot
of crackpots!
I'm elated...
until she sees no real money
in my powerful hand,
or even the other one...
But of course,
I must NEVER stop the words!
They are my soul, in case,
I don't already know.

Flip, flip...
Devils, fools, women in chains...
I relate instantly and wait –
she'll know I'm broken,
homeless of heart and any intention.

.../cont.

Instead,
I'm assured my home is wonderful,
my heart is secured forever...
(those bloody chains I surmise.)

Flip, flip...
Am I aware I have three children?
An old soul with his head screwed
on correctly according to the laws
of...screwed on heads...
A studious middle child with
potential to design rocket ships
(albeit glad for anything less significant,
as slightly uninspired.)
A daughter who has taken my throne,
along with my man's heart.
Well I never! (Snigger, sigh again.)

Flip, flop...
But you know,
I *am* going to leave
something,
as she says...
Her,
with a sense of heightened humour
and these words
she in fact gifted me,
and the definite realization of
just how talented
I've become,
at knowing how to bullshit
the bullshit artist.

MS. CONFIGURED

I no longer leave my home;
with renewed conviction,
every day I try.
I would have to get dressed,
and although I stare
at an eclectic collection of garments,
I'd rather climb within and simply
wrap a scarf around my neck,
than try to configure any
of my old self on my new body.

*Her complexion mostly blue,
her gift wrapping,
in hues...*

CHECKING OUT

Busy schedule,
mid-life.
Suddenly seems
I MUST
check my:
eyes,
ears,
boobs,
vagina,
blood,
moles...
Anything left between?

After,
some small yet
unwelcome polyps
are extradited
from my cervix,
I'm told,
to swallow pills
the size of
not-so-small
fortunate countries.
I'm simply chuffed,
they forgot to check
my pulse.

Roll up your sleeves, no one has time to see your heart.

GOING UNDER

You're a stranger,
I've known forever.
Nothing left to say,
everything unspoken.
Lack lustre,
brilliance now shining in progeny.

Even your breath
exasperates,
syphons entity until
my lungs give in.
I thought by now we'd be sailing...
When did we start
going under?

*Remind me
I am the love of your life
so it feels less likely,
it's passing us by....*

Rebellious

PUSSY WHIPPED

He does
as he's told
on repeat;
memory
as long
as it is short.
Her exasperation
futile as
his efforts
to remember.

He's whipped
alright,
but only
momentarily.
The sofa
groans each time
he recalls,
she howls
for always the same
reason.

*If I keep allowing your blatant ignorance to hurt me,
irony would have it, I am the stupid one.*

TAKE NOTE

Had you still looked at me
as though my lips unlocked
the secret to eternal life;
listened attentively as though
I was unravelling ancient codes.
Even once, made comment that
I hold the beauty of a timeless
screen-siren,
I may not have delighted in him
devouring my every morsel
with the rapture of a hungry scholar,
whilst yet again, the headmaster,
failed to take note.

Don't feign surprise, disintegration was all too evident.
Sirens pealed, smoke signalled fire.
Burying your head in the ashes of our demise, does little
to clear you of perpetration.

Rebellious

DANGLING

I dangle,
you watch.

My feet
kick dust.

You fail
to react.

You don't
extend.

My safety-net
waits.

Lips pursed,
ready to blow.

*You don't write anymore,
you've never time to speak
and I'm tired of straining my eyes,
only to hear nothing.*

DREAMCATCHER

Even in dreams
you're so elusive;
last night
you came to me
as a man with no
legs.
I guess that's one way
of making sure
you can't leave.

*While there's still a glimmer
you will return,
I've learned to warm myself.*

AWAKE AT DAWN

You
found
me
in places
untouched
as only
strangers do
when
you awaken
at dawn
naked
inside them.

*You left just enough space,
to romanticise the hollow.*

Eye candy
soul food
sweet fancy
sustenance

or

divine spiritual
nourishment
you're mine
to devour
and Boy
I'm ravenous

ON A WHIM

This
foreign tongue
you bring
opens borders,
makes me click
Spanish heels,
strip-tease
around Big Ben,
skinny-dip
in the Thames.

Keep talking;
French kiss
your words,
pour me
English Breakfast.
I'm not
accustomed
to waking up
on a whim
such as this.

*I knew you before,
another time,
we didn't yet know.
Aloof yet in order,
perfect conditions,
precisely unknown.*

JE T'AIME

Your pillow lips
were custom-made
for mine to lay upon.
Cushioned in desire,
resting assured
they were only designed
to part, for the intrusion
of fervent tongues.

I simply needed your caress;
you tickled my fancy.

Rebellious

LOVE REVOLUTION

I never knew
the precision in desire
until you unlocked
my covert secrets
with one
revolutionary turn
of your rogue tongue.

*Your bee-stung lips, pollen to my nectar.
Liquid lust tonic, sugar-sweet elixir;
syrup of the Gods.*

LEAVE IT TO THE BREEZE

You tried
so hard
not to notice
the way
my dress
parted
between
my thighs,
but I knew
soon,
we'd just
leave it all
to the breeze.

I found
you
in the sky;
elusive,
unreachable,
holding
promise.

©Leanne Neill
LUST for WORDS

SIZE EIGHT

I've made some stupid choices
in the name of middle age.
No doubt you were one;
though risk begot words,
gain weighs heavier than loss.
I've kissed size eight goodbye;
my mind is just too full now,
to squeeze into you.

*You appeared;
mortal sin
draped celestially
in a sheath
of unholy desire.*

JUST A SMALL PRICK

Ponytail pulled
excruciatingly
tight,
strategically
positioned,
hardened bangs.

One small syringe,
liquid life-line:
negating
all need
for any such
concealed tension.

*She learned to bask in the glory of her wisdom,
having already spent years hiding
the insignificance of her beauty.*

SELFLESS (LOOK AT ME)

Doe eyes,
poised lips,
open just slightly
to suggestion.
Angled from above,
hints of promise
in cleaves of curvature.
Filtered to deconstruct;
unwanted realities,
blurring lines
of imperfection.
Darling,
you're not
fooling anyone;
except yourself.

I much prefer
young at heart
over
immature;
my heart
has surely
come of age,
tolerated
all seasons,
settled decisively,
in spring.

ONLY WOMEN BLEED

Boring
all these
sugar-coated
words,
love, devotion
and such
inane stuff.

I prefer
acrid talk
about things
that bleed
and hurt,
like women
and men.

*I listen with ears shaped by disillusion,
keeping in mind I still hear a semblance
of hope.*

SCRAMBLED EGGS

As those
last live eggs
banshee to the virility
of his barefaced
bloom,
I recall I've never been
quite expert,
at separating my heartbeat
from a joke.

I may have been lost according to the laws of morality,
but for the first time in my life,
I followed my heart.
I make no apologies.

Rebellious

TAKE YOUR PICK

She can take you
to heaven
or leave you
in hell;
all
or
nothing,

no in-between.

Purgatory
merely
a waiting room
for the meek,
who fail
to choose
an extreme.

Troubled by my reflection, hazy recognition.
I knew her once; before she had issues with God,
rejected all institution by self-intervention.
She confuses me with her new complexion,
but damn, she's exquisite.

SCARS

I
marked
my skin
today,
in permanent
ink.

I
always
wanted you
to believe
I was cool.

I
wasn't quite
brave enough,
to use
a knife.

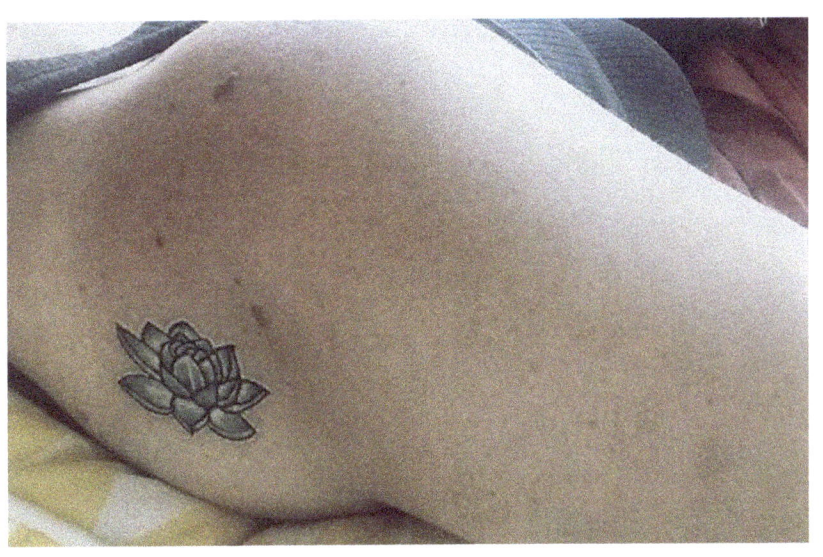

Rebellious

GOTHIC LOVE

Dyed
your hair
at midnight,
changed clothes
to reflect.
Inked your arm
before the dawn,
then asked
if I could still
find you
sexy
painted black.

In the decay of darkness lies the shadow of light.

Rebellious

DON'T CALL ME BABY

Touch her body
as you did mine.
Speak to her,
those same words.
Call her *Baby*,
loathed that anyway;
always you,
acting the child.

We're all just one
shiny Casanova away
from finding our knight
in rusty armour.
Days then slowly corroding,
tarnished by second-hand
valour.

*Keep reminding me you're all shiny and new,
as though it was my choice you gifted this to someone else,
when it was me who loved you damaged.*

Rebellious

SHOULD KNOW BETTER

On the corner,
looked straight
through;
sullen, foreboding,
much like you.

I fell into him,
just the same.

*Sometimes love simply
has no intention
of conforming to convention.*

BUCKLE UP

If only
you came
with safety
precautions,
warnings,
like other
turbulent
adventures:

seat belt,
brace position,
oxygen mask,
life vest...

emergency exit
highly recommended
before takeoff...

*Watch how I walk
with eloquence and grace,
from the height
of your audacity.*

Rebellious

THE BIGGEST FOOL

You tapped me
on the nose,
condescending,
covered in cute.

You're learning,
you said...

I knew exactly
which of us
was in fact,
the greater fool.

I loved you enough to know, I wasn't.

EVASION

Surely
it's intuitively
on the cards,
balance of my stars,
phase of a crystal moon,
lap of a male god,
straw in my martini?
Circling surety
that evades
my wanting fingers.

JAMBALAYA

It's a jumble
my head,
some might say
a *mind-fuck*
of stupid
proportions.
His kisses
so light,
yours so hard;
my tongue
trying to regulate
both
to suit
my palate
as I serve
our dinner
cold.

*Because when he kisses me
he tastes nothing
like you...*

DEMONS

We tip-toe
with trepidation
around your demons,
conquered and strewn.
All too aware,
in true stories of horror,
they always
rise again.

*I'm no scribe of fairies and fantasy,
only the reality of demons
that truly exist.*

TIGHTROPE

I'm not of this world,
though I don't rise above.
Can't quite commit to the pretentious set,
let alone settle for mediocrity;
neither the funds
nor the composition, either way.
I'm on a trampoline
bounding between purgatorial
highs and lows.
A trapeze artist
bluffing balance of the fine wire.
The reality;
they are wide and slippery with the grease
of convention.
I slip and I slide,
waiting for my circus to arrive;
knowing full well even then,
I've not the courage to run.

*She'd rather hunger for a perilous adventure,
than starve on the safety of routine.*

FUCK YOU

Your banality,
need to appease
your throbbing
vagina
while you pretend
to revere all
our Sisters
fought for
in the name
of autonomy,
makes me want
to scream.

*Flattering myself
has become
my pleasure.*

UNFOUND

How are you?
Meaning it...
Let's catch up soon.
Seriously...

Chasing, chasing.
No longer bothered;
people don't want
to be found.

Don't try to find me.
I've gone; that place you say my head always resides.
At least now I accept it's where I belong.
I'm going to unpack there.

Rebellious

SUPERFICIAL BY ASSOCIATION

I do feel
a sense
of injustice;
she tells me
her Mercedes
has been knifed
yet again,
they're
struggling
to find a moor
for their boat
on the coast.

Mostly though,
I'm disturbed
at the way
she pisses me off
by constantly
flicking her hair.

She carries a Target dress as though it's Chanel.
She never cared much anyway
for being labelled.

Rebellious

COSTUME CHANGE

Wearing people
as costume jewellery,
changeable
as your mind.

Tugging strings,
instigating tension,
until each one breaks,
proving they are
dispensable.

*Writing my invisible lines of hope
in between
the wait
of your
every considered
pause...*

PINK BITS

China blue faces,
delicate minds.
The weaker sex?
Indeed!

Slaying
testosterone
carelessly
into flimsy pink.

I dipped my toe in your attention.
Both feigning ignorance to the game;
you would devour all ten,
I would swallow you whole.

POSTCARDS

Corporations measure her worth
in millilitres.
There's a price on her face,
barcode on her forehead,
Use by date,
stamped on her demeanour.
All in the terminology though
it seems;
Best before,
may soften the blow.

Society is fickle,
there's still money to be made;
just a different set of insecurities to target.
Discarding all receipts, proof of value,
she sends postcards from her lustrous heart.
She knows despite her sunscreen,
she's just beginning to ripen.
There are few, can afford her...

*If you're going to sell your soul for free,
at least charge for your pussy.*

DRESS CODE: CASUAL

Everyone stared,
I admit, so did I.
Who does that?
Not even possible
to mistake
for other casual attire.
Perhaps at least
a lacy gown
could double
as a dress?

Scanning her milk,
I understand
the morning urgency
in discovering
none for my coffee.
I take my fucking
judgement hat off,
(I'm always overdressed)
to the lady
in pyjamas.

Nothing can't be achieved if you turn to face the stars and poke your tongue at the universe.

BOOM

Incessant ticking;
mind, heart, clock...
Missed the boat;
so many times, different ports.
Through the motions, déjà vu.
Stepford wife, domestic goddess,
robotic housemaid;
sans romanticism, pay cheque.
Resentful heart, sincere intention.
Smile through contempt,
only self to blame.
Privileged princess without a tiara.
Pretend to be something;
anything but yourself.
Just waiting for the
B O O M....

Every word entwined with fibres of you,
fraying in neglect of me.

Rebellious

BECOMING

Becoming;
middle-aged
woman.

Resenting
every rule
held true,
reconsidering
every thought
owned,
questioning
every belief
entrenched.

Not only
swaying
on edge,
throwing
herself
over.

*I've not evolved, merely reverted into who I always was,
before conditioned just to be.*

SQUEEZE BOX

Squeezing into your box;
I don't fit.
Can't speak in tongues
that only make sense to the elite few,
my script too simple.
No doubt I get by with a pretty face,
under the guise of artistic licence.
Possible flashes of brilliance
doused by commercialism,
an ego that refuses to bow to critique.
I never claimed to be anyone special,
let alone Plath or Poe.
Just a composer of words
for the simple of heart,
and I sure as hell don't recall,
begging for yours.

*Always a square peg,
redefining her fit.*

CAN'T KEEP A GOOD WOMAN DOWN

You can't
burst my bubble...

I blew it
from lips of steel,
with whimsy,
soap and super-glue.

It's bound
to me by carefully
mastered strings,
of ascending power.

*On some days she conquered the world,
on others, she succumbed to the rest.*

AND TRUTH IS STRANGER THAN POETRY

I'm a writer;
always handy
for that
interview question:
Tell me
something interesting
about yourself...
and initially
it is,
though your readers
imaginary,
your real ones few,
and their eyes glaze
like those cherries
you always hated
when you specify
poetry
and they raise
their penciled brows
if they still can,
and throw you
a cringe worthy rhyme
at which
you obligingly giggle
because
your rent is overdue,
kick your own shins
and remember
next time
you'll just say,
I have a pet donkey!

RIPPLES (FOR CHARLOTTE)

Reposing,
she tells me
I look like a fish.
Okay,
I have before
been likened
to salmon;
apparently
we all resemble
an animal.

Flitting away
unaware,
I gurgle quietly.
With her orange
eye-shadow,
my little Nemo.

ALL THAT I AM

Her black
is always
darkest,
she tells me
I must be *tough*;
another way to say,
*Don't trouble me
with yours...*

Little does
she realise,
I know
her efforts
to quell my spirit
while still inside,
and for all that,
I am.

*Of course, you never understand as a child...
How the friction of weary bones
leads to inhalation of particles
your ancestors left in their wake.*

GROWING PAIN

Always
a strangeness;
soul that defied
its time,
grappling
to conform,
frivolity
of youth.
A deeper sense
than just being,
melancholy love
for all that hurt;
as though pain
was worth living,
all grown up.

As the sun, she will rise...

FORCE OF NATURE

They take
flowers,
force them
into colours
unintended
through a straw
to the absurd
which we suck on
with
oohs and aahs,
but I do wonder
how
they really feel...

Dishevelled
I don't do well
clouded in
the good shape
of nine —
happy.

COMMON COLD

I'm so sick
of know-all
life coaches,
pumped
personal trainers,
colourful
anti-depressants,
5 ingredients
self-help books,
pragmatic affirmations,
flirtations with saviours,
hysterical acquaintances,
plastic magicians;
breathing purposefully
through a blocked nose
and not feeling
better.

Bitter, this futile taste I can't scrape;
white-coat surrender, biting inside my head.

ALMOST REPENTANT

Slap in the face
you didn't see
coming
when long
dawn arrives
and you're
reeling
around yourself –

remorse.

AMEN

Most dislike
their mother-in-law,
except me.
Mine is wise,
stoically abides
by the order
of our Lord.

Adept at turning
at least one eye
to my indifference,
she told me once,
*look after your relationship,
or when your children leave
there'll be nothing left.*

So, as we sit
across a platter to share,
little to say
that's not mildly encased in
skin of our fruitful loins,
laced in strychnine tankards
of our ailing business,
or resentfully held in vessels
of being the better-half...

I concede,
there probably is a God.

FML

I'm no fun
anymore,
though the
greater part
is hysterical.

Sipping tears
with a smile,
completely
fucking
ambiguous.

*Such stillness now,
sands suspended
in this non-missing
inertia.*

REVERIE OF YOUTH

Black dress,
stiletto heels,
music pumping,
bodies in rhythm.
Spy the one
catches your eye,
careless whispers,
flirtatious laughter,
cocktail illusions,
lost inhibitions.
Endless nights
unbothered by morning;
tomorrow repeats
without regret.
Reverie of youth.
I can hardly
remember...

*Her reality may be black and white,
but she certainly still dreams in colour.*

SURVIVAL OF THE FITTEST

They
never tell us
the real
reason
we need to stay
fit.

Infinite hoops
to climb through,
always entangling.
Tenacious obstacles
to move,
strategically positioned.
Persistent hurdles,
varying levels
we must leap.

At the end,
it's a conspiracy
of respiratory
proportions;
we all end up
out of breath.

*Poets put so much energy into their words,
perhaps there is scarcely any left,
for the exhausting task of realism.*

TIME DOESN'T WAIT

Bus driver did warn,
fatality ahead;
but we all know
human nature kills
more than just cats,
and though the carcass
lay strewn,
respectfully covered,
my heart catapulted
straight to the knock,
the mother,
the hardened cop:
*Your son, I'm sorry,
afraid he is dead.*
I marveled
at the Asian couple,
didn't pause their conversation,
(even to take photographs),
no one else
lifted their gaze.
It was just me
and that body
watching,
as the world
passed us by.

Limbs
torn apart
sucked in
marrow
heart
dangling
irrepressible
thread
of sinew —

disjointed.

MISSING ME

I miss myself.
The me that laughed
without contrivance,
danced without constriction.
Friends that shared revelry,
before responsibility;
uncertainty over conviction.
I long to be nonchalant,
over necessary.

Precious —
time you spend
when
you have it…

Don't think
I haven't noticed
it's dependent
on you -
choosing myself.

FOREVER IS SHORT

Does it echo
as you lay
your head,
hers beside
yours?

That intrusive,
rhythmic,
God-forsaken
recognition...

I want you,
forever.

Apparently, our love could survive all wars
except one with brown eyes,
camouflaged in surrender.

Almost Repentant

OLD IS NEW

I'd never
seen her name
before,
at least,
not in these times.
Now a neon sign
wherever I go...
keyrings,
jackets,
bed linen,
your smile.
Mocking
my ignorance
to the newness
of things
no longer old,
like me.

She looks lovely dressed in my goodbye.

CRUCIFIXION

It was warm
when you
handed it,
saying
it was mine,
but
it dripped through
my fingers,
her palms
they were cupped,
and still
I taste your truth,
licking
my wounds,
chewing
on nails.

*My mind moves faster than my hand,
so when I make a mess of*

I LOVE YOU,

please know my conscience is clear. X

C'EST LA VIE

He's a world away.
He's a girl away.
He's a lifetime gone by.

She misses him.
She's jealous of her.
She regrets

all
that can't be
recovered.

I promised I'd never allow another to make me cry,
but I wrapped him in your skin,
watched the layers peel
and then I wondered why...

PURGE

I need to
spill my guts,
until
you no longer question
what's inside.

I was thin ten years ago.
The kind of skinny
other women resent;
when they tell you to eat up,
cause you look so bad.
I wondered if they were genuine,
until a herd of hormones
I'd only ever read about
came to tell me I no longer had
a choice to wonder,
and curves were the new
thigh-gap I had to embrace.

It chafes and grates,
every day,
as my reflection
battles self-love versus self-loathe.
I don't know who to begrudge,
the people vindicated
because they told me so,
or the mirror
that says it's okay to succumb now,
to emaciated bones, I no longer own.

Not until she lost her quest for perfection
she realised
she was simply beautiful.

WASTING TIME

I've been spending
so much time
measuring
the circumference
of my upper arms
and thighs,
I failed to notice
the way
my new curves
accentuate the size
of my heart.

It's everything,
yet nothing.
All we have,
more we don't -
time.

DEFUNCT

I feel
my womb
shrivelling,
weeping orifices
provide
no rehydration.

My
hips and thighs
thickening;
some kind of
unnecessary
rebellion.

As if
my head
is not
already heavy,
just holding
itself up.

*We get angry as we bleed out,
how the world still pirouettes around the ones
we never knew we once were.*

Beauty
never wanes,
we become
idle.
The longer
we look,
the less
we see.

AGE OLD QUESTIONS

How will I know
when I don't turn you on?

When my sensuality disfigures,
morphs into that old lady
you despise.

When they're flitting around you,
shining their tight bodies,
loose minds.

When I'm forgetting who I am
and you're just learning yourself.

Always;
seems only a matter of time.

*Love at first sight is one thing,
love that lasts the entire view is another...*

CAMEO APPEARANCE

You left
for the
first half,
came back
in the second
just in case
I'd missed
your show,
but it must
always go on
as they say,
despite
difficult children,
wild animals,
and I'll take
your cameo
as a token
of my
professionalism.

*If you feel the need to stand in my light,
better you know,
I'm tired of sharing.*

Almost Repentant

HAPPILY UNBOTHERED

There's a certain
tranquillity
in being
unbothered...

opening
the front door
any hour
in my nightgown,
only trees rustling
slight disapproval.

Indulgence
in time
to formulate problems
into equations
that don't add up.

A reliable man
who stays quiet,
appreciates all
I've managed to keep
together;
bring to the table

despite offspring
who'll ask
What's for dinner?
with a scowl
they prepared earlier.

Outside the perimeter
they'll have me believe
I'm counterproductive.

It's quite possible
they are simply jealous,
and I'm just afraid,
I'm happy...

*I see my breath today
in a mist of disillusion
refusing to disperse
into the blue...*

Almost Repentant

SONDER

Much
speculation
about the location
of home,
spare me
the emotives,
people and hearts.

Hometowns
hold only
regret,
in between,
friends for life
no longer
bothering
with now.

As I meld
into the seams
of buildings,
alleys
that bind together
those who
no longer lift
their eyes
to see -

this sonder
feeling,
so close...

N✺THING NEW

I need
to trust
my gut;
how it churns
on spin cycle,
s l o w i n g
to a grinding halt.
W o o z y,
wrung dry
by the
repetition,
repetition
of your
predictability.

You arrived,
back wanting the me you no longer needed,
glistening sweat
of her prized futility
still adorning your mouth.

To nail
her
simply
turn her
palms
and use
the template
of those
came before -

martyr.

IT'S IN THE BAG

She asks if I have
a special occasion,
almost seems
a conversation worth having.
I pull out my rehearsed
winning quip,
life itself is one!
She chuckles on cue
as though I'm funny,
but hey,
I've already denied
red espadrilles in restraint,
my humour is low.

There's undeniable existence
in consumerism,
comradery in this therapy,
forgery in the currency.
Indoor palms and fraudulent heat
allude to paradise,
though children in melt-down
should be excluded in favour
of designer margaritas.
Surely, I can't be alone
in going home to unpack
yet another empty handbag.

APOLOGY TO MY CHILDREN

Forgive me child.
I swear it felt safe
when I made that decision,
years ago,
in the name of selfish validation.
God damn, procreation.

It was before
the planes hit,
bombs blasted,
innocent blood shed,
and we watched
hatred live;
hands and knees folding
as it plays out,
over and over...

*Your first exhalation, my expiration.
Stench of resent;
thick with all I let go,
for an existence you don't want.*

BLACK DOG NIPPING

Incessant barking
slicing the luxury
of today's
silence,
succumbing
to a howl...
and I need
not look
any further
beyond the barrier
to know for sure,
it is black.

*Annie Lennox always knew,
when time is reversed
it turns black,
and the rain,
it comes again...*

HAPPY PILL

Why is it not
remotely amusing,
aesthetically pleasing,
more palatable?

Smiley-stamped,
purple polka-dotted,
fairy-floss flavoured;
giggling on the way down...

Indigestible,
gagging reflexes,
sticking in my throat.
The hair of a stranger;
promising grin.
I believe, I must swallow.

*Just another day we say.
The only big deal in mundanity
is surviving...*

We all
want it
badly,
so much so
when we
say never again,
our hearts are
already
peeping around
the next corner –
love.

PASSING THE TIME

I loathe
that time
will tell...

It speaks
too much;
whispers
all I've wasted,
declares
no refunds,
gossips
all errors.

Professes
little hope,
of you.

I've always wanted men I can't have.
If love isn't torture,
I don't feel it.

THE ONE

One
stays with you
as life spirals by,
visits in technicolor;
rapid eye movements.
Beats your heart,
right out of your chest.
Comes to the fore
of every thought,
tucked in back.
Turns you on,
when all has expired.
Elevates above any,
floating in your peripheral.
Smack bang centre
The love of your life.

*From trying to forget,
to smiling when I remember,
our memory now spun
full circle.*

EYE OF THE BEHOLDER

You're annoyed –
just loudly
for a change,
and though
it's all
in the name of art,
you should remember
it was you,
chose
not to see it.

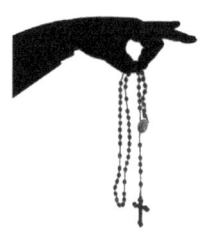

The fairy tale begins when she fits her own slipper.

THE HARD WAY

She's an
experiential
learner.
Some call it
The hard way,
but she prefers
long-winded
enlightenment –
sometimes
there is just
no time or space
for meandering
pussies.

Effortless it seems,
the way she sashays words onto the page...

MY CONFESSION

I can't pinpoint my revolt.
It was long after
I belligerently refused church,
anointing my mother
empowerment
to reprimand me for wasting
all her dollars
on Catholic tuition.

For years after,
the ingrained bellow
of indoctrination
kept me fearful enough
to continue mindless
unquestioning –
the only God,
I was ever allowed to know.

*Calling on angels,
any that can sever our cord;
ties that bind us together forcibly,
against all human resistance.*
(REIKI)

INTENTS AND PURPOSE

Changed the sheets,
vacuumed the floor;
few spare moments
between selling dresses
as though I care...
sitting at a table
of familiar strangers
trying not to worry
that those
other bastards
still want to take me
to the cleaners
and for all
intents and purpose,
pretending
I'm still the one
in control.

*If she tells you where to go,
you will ask politely
for directions.*

CHARITY

I'd watch you
weep
at starving
Africans,
thirsty farmers...

Maybe this
time,
you'd put
your hand
in your pocket?

But holy water
was enough
to console all suffering,
including
your own –

and I learned
when daughters
grow into their mothers,
compassion is more
than you'd ever shown.

*I wonder if an unforgiving heart
omits its own errors?*

LOW RESOLUTION

Along
with Sydney
train lines'
New Year's Eve
she's shutting down,
rescheduling.
Regulars get off,
foreigners board.
Buckling in predestined
heat,
derailing in platform
conformity.
Only one conductor
foretells direction
but he looks
like her father,
and he no longer
knows.
Never mind;
she lives
in Melbourne.

I can't hear if you're breathing, you're so far away...
STILL
I can feel you whispering softly, from your distance.

DERMAL BIOGRAPHY

Dermal biography of life;
atlas of bound topographic lines.
Three furrowed forehead tracks,
worn by insolent offspring.
Fault lines forming between eyes;
epicentre of guilt, contempt.
Crinkly cornered optic globes,
creases of absurdity over time.
Perimeter around down-turned lips,
the scars of missing yours....

Some days perfect kernels,
almond eyes,
others,
the corrugated shell.

HOME

I thought
it was grand,
that old house.
We laughed;
if Dad kept
painting the boards,
the car would
no longer
fit in the driveway.

Never mind icicles
hanging from my nose,
a bedroom
of concrete walls.
The living-room
made up for it,
scorching my socks
as I lay my feet to melt
on the fireplace door.

Eighties laminate
kitchen renovation,
my make-believe café.
Servery,
double-door pantry,
sized perfectly
for hide and seek;
Mum's Lamingtons*
squishing
between my toes.

.../cont.

Dad's cellar of intrigue,
mouldy cheese and salami.
Friends jovially
downing homemade wine
in white singlets
only *real men* wore
with dress pants.

Vegetable field
come vineyard,
backyard,
fruit orchard,
spilling out front.

Chickens let loose
beadily watching
the crazy lady
occasionally surfacing
to take their eggs
or their lives,
in the quest
for good broth.

I pondered
the ghosts…
who passed
under that roof?
Were they swinging
on white lace
curtain whispers
as I slept,
and how now
my family
left it,
still breathing
for someone else
to wonder.

*Lamingtons are an Australian sponge cake, coated in chocolate and rolled in coconut.

FATHER CHRISTMAS

Christmas
has dispersed;
children,
laughter,
table of strangers
unwrapped.
Along with
Santa Claus,
my father
doesn't remember
me.

NEVER MATTER

Eyes baptized
in reunion,
limbs entwined
in homecoming.

Rain obliging,
ordered ode
to perfection.

364 days now.
I have relived
your departure
in each thirsty drop.

*The more time and distance between us,
the longer
we never mattered.*

Almost Repentant

ODE TO MEN O PAUSE

You
surround
yourself
with people

nothing
between
their ears

getting by
with what lies
between
their legs

all bitching
about
ex-husbands
at fault

that your head
is empty
and your vagina
knows better

I scratch
their surface
watch the Stupid
rise in a puff

of twenty smug
womanising
ejaculators

.../cont.

but you feel
clever
because
they all wanted

to get inside
your
vacancy sign

and he
was just
trying
to love you.

I know your body is with hers.
I know your heart is with mine.

Her arms
a new cloak
of salvation.
Open wide;
you collapse
into a similar
shape of me.

SOFT FALL

Deafening
this time –
you took
my words,
gave them
to her,
and though
I'm giving
mine
to him,
I miss
the softness
that was once
our
silence.

*At a place never thought I'd be;
where your memory resides but falls like leaves,
and each day missing, turns sparse.*

Almost Repentant

THE CRASH

Sucker
for a fixer-upper.
Foundation
always solid,
all else
merely
cosmetic adjustments.

Heart strings
would pull,
pink purse strings
open.
She'd overcapitalise,
he'd underinvest,
everything un hinge

and though
he claimed
to be a handyman,
location
indeed perfect,
she'd never groan
exactly how
she'd imagined....

and he'd always
hand it to himself
in the end.

*She'll always give herself away,
then wonder why she's empty.*

Spiralling,
d
i
z
z
y
in the vortex.
On the cusp
of gripping
rationality,
surrendering
to the
h o l l o w.

PHOENIX

Dispel
our memory,
relegate it
to the ashes
of ancient
mythology.

Rise;
build myself
a new empire
founded on
purity
of truth.

Honour
thyself;
nobility
is in my own
actuality.

*No one is as beautifully cursed,
as a poet.*

SURRENDER

You've still
time,
pry me
from his arms;
they've not yet
entirely circled...

but you're standing,
white shirt,
hands
in the air,
and I can only
wave back

goodbye.

*If you're not going to work to keep her,
don't apply.*

THE LIGHT

Maybe it's time
to relent;
to a higher power.
I'm messing it all up
with the consistency
of a prodigal fool.
My supremacy of self
a well-constructed fallacy,
all outside saviours,
devils in obvious disguise.
In foetal position,
I'll await your voice;
same one came to me years ago,
in the darkness of a child lost.
She told me that everything
was going to be just fine;
like any wise woman,
she was right.
Come to me
my guardian angel,
I'll not denounce you this time.
Please tell me again;
I'm ready now,
for the light.

She absolves,
tries to forget,
continues
to make allowances,
gets little
to nothing
back.
It's her turn now,
no more concessions -

justify my love.

LONG SERVICE LEAVE

Sabbatical
of sorts,
leave
without pay.
Sojourn
in silence,
forgotten
my baggage.
One of us
let go;
my head,
it is empty.

I see you peeking; can't be easy to hide your light.
Uninspired, seeking restoration in obscure places.

Almost Repentant

POET'S DEPARTURE LOUNGE

You say,
*Don't stop
writing.*

I say,
*Don't stop
surviving*

and like
wishes
we flicker

with
promises
so thin

they
can't help
but extinguish.

*Like a dying
romance,
its last throes;
fake enthusiasm,
make a little sound.
All the words
slip away...*

FINAL PRAYER

If it wasn't the bottle
going down,
it was euphoria
up in smoke.
If not your words,
his lyrics,
if not my him,
your her.

Now
it's that cross
you're bearing.
I just want to lay
with you
and pray;
finally,
it's my turn.

As I lay
I almost
retracted;
necessity
for something
familiar
in promise –
    prayer.

BIOGRAPHICAL NOTE

Leanne Neill is a creative fashion stylist, mother of three, and a self-professed 'composer of words.' She has over twenty years of experience in public libraries and local government. In 2016, she started her poetry and art inspired Facebook page : LUST for WORDS, and has since been published in many ezines and pages including Spillwords , Bymepoetry, including their WOMb anthology, The Scarlet Leaf Review, Blue Nib, Raven Cage, Husk Magazine, and US anthologies, Dandelion in a Vase of Roses and Warriors With Wings. Her first collection, Fine Lines and Unpolished Pieces of Me was published by TAT Publishing in 2017. Her second poetry collection, Blue Lotus was released in June, 2018. Leanne lives in Melbourne, Australia.

Find her at :
Facebook.com/LUST-for-WORDS
Instagram : lust_for_words_by_leanne_neill

www.ingramcontent.com/pod-product-compliance
Lightning Source LLC
Chambersburg PA
CBHW042116100526
44587CB00025B/4080